OLD AGE COMES
AT A BAD TIME

OLD AGE COMES AT A BAD TIME

Wit and Wisdom for the Young at Heart

Selected and Introduced by
Eliakim Katz

Stoddart

Published in 1997 by Stoddart Publishing Co. Limited
34 Lesmill Road, Toronto, Canada M3B 2T6

Distributed in Canada by General Distribution Services Limited
34 Lesmill Road, Toronto, Canada M3B 2T6
Tel. (416) 445-3333   Fax (416) 445-5967
Email Customer.Service@ccmailgw.genpub.com

Distributed in the U.S. by General Distribution Services Inc.
85 River Rock Drive, Suite 202, Buffalo, New York 14207
Toll-free tel. 1-800-805-1083   Toll-free fax 1-800-481-6207
Email gdsinc@genpub.com

01 00 99 98 97   1 2 3 4 5

Cataloging in Publication Data

Main entry under title:
Old age comes at a bad time: wit and wisdom for the young at heart

ISBN 0-7737-5929-8

1. Old age - Quotations, maxims, etc.   2. Aging - Quotations, maxims, etc.
3. Old age - Humor.   4. Aging - Humor.   I. Katz, Eliakim.

PN6084.05042 1997   808.88'2   97-931651-0

Text design: Tannice Goddard

Printed in Canada

Page 97 constitutes a continuation of the copyright page.

To my wife, Stella,
who keeps me as young as possible under the circumstances,
and to my father, Shlomo,
who is living proof that old age need not be a bad time

Kimberley Glaze typed much of the manuscript and managed, more than once, to retrieve text from electronic oblivion; Laura Siberry, my editor at Stoddart, was always patient, encouraging, and insightful. I wish to thank them both.

Introduction

Two years ago I was at a lakeside trying to negotiate a speed-boat ride for my daughter and two of my nieces. The man I was haggling with quoted an outrageous price. Taken by surprise I said, "How much?"

"What's the matter, Pops," he said, "losing your hearing also?"

"Pops? POPS!? Do I look like a Pops?" I thought. "And what does he mean by also?" I bent over and, Narcissus style, looked at my reflection in the water. He was right. Peter Pan was nowhere to be seen. Sardonic middle age looked up at me from the water. You are getting old, Father William.

For years I had been brushing aside hair loss, closing my eyes to an increasing tendency to read at arm's length, and making little of the fact that (so far) two of my children are taller than me. But denial can only be taken so far. My hair is joining the hair of my father (baldness is my "hairitage"), I now need bifocals, and my son must bend down to kiss me. With the four on my odometer being gently but firmly edged out by the five and with "Pops" ringing in my ears, I have finally begun to accept that getting older is not something that only happens to other people. I have seen the future, and it is aging.

And, of course, there is no respite or hiding from it. I am getting older as I write this, and you are not getting any younger as you read it. Whatever we do, our aging keeps staring us in the face. It is the constant in our lives, and the years are the only real measure of our journey.

Aging is about losing our youth and finding a varicose vein. It is about fighting our children and making peace with our parents. It is about reflecting on the past, thinking of the future, and facing our mortality. It is about changing mental and physical capacities and hormone replacement therapy. It is about gaining wisdom and mislaying our reading glasses. It is about how we want to be remembered and what we want to forget.

Throughout time, people have feared aging, laughed at it, cried about it, defied it, accepted it — and written about it.

From the irony of Oscar Wilde to the gentle poetry of Emily Dickinson, from the one-liners of George Burns to the playful verse of Ogden Nash, from the drama of Shakespeare to the humour of Jerry Seinfeld, there is something for everyone in this collection of responses to the inevitable, irreversible, but not necessarily unpleasant effects of getting older.

By Way of a
Half-hearted Apology

To the people I have cited
Both living and dead:
I have borrowed your words,
But they *are* being read.

And if I have misquoted,
Or mis-spelt a name:
Accept my regrets
My errors — my shame.

— *Eliakim Katz*

How confusing the beams from memory's lamp are;
One day a bachelor, the next a grampa.
What is the secret of the trick?
How did I get so old so quick?
— *Ogden Nash*

Old age is the most unexpected of all the things
that happen to a man.
— *Leon Trotsky*

If you don't want to get old,
hang yourself while young.
— *Jewish proverb*

I knew a man who gave up smoking, drinking, sex, and food. He was healthy right up to the time he killed himself.
— *Johnny Carson*

*T*he secret of staying young is to live honestly, eat slowly, and lie about your age.
— *Lucille Ball*

*W*e can't reach old age by another man's road. My habits protect my life, but they would assassinate you.
— *Mark Twain*

I have everything now that I had twenty years ago,
except now it's all lower.
— *Gypsy Rose Lee (exotic dancer)*

*M*y health is good;
it's my age that's bad.
— *Ray Acuff*

*O*ld age isn't for sissies.
— *Bette Davis*

*W*hen a man falls into his anecdotage,
it is a sign for him to retire.
— *Benjamin Disraeli*

*T*he "good old times":
all times, when old, are good.
— *Lord Byron*

*A*n archeologist is the best husband any woman can have; the older she gets, the more interested he is in her.
— *Agatha Christie*

*W*henever a man's friends begin to compliment him about looking young, he may be sure they think he is getting old.
— *Washington Irving*

*I*nside every seventy-year-old is a thirty-five-year-old asking, "What happened?"
— *Ann Landers*

*H*e who laughs, lasts.
— *Mary Pettibone Poole*

*M*iddle age — when you begin to smile at things
that used to cause you to laugh.
— *Puck's magazine*

*T*hings do not change,
we do.
— *Henry David Thoreau*

*N*o memory of having starred
Atones for later disregard,
Or keeps the end from being hard.
— *Robert Frost*

*T*he apparent serenity of the past is an oil spread by time.
— *Lloyd Frankenberg*

*O*ld age is life's unsafe harbour.
— *Elliott Priest*

$\mathcal{Y}$ou know you're old when you notice
how young the derelicts are getting.
— *Jeanne Phillips*

$\mathcal{I}$ am an old man
and have known
many troubles,
but most of them
never happened.
— *Mark Twain*

Old age comes at a bad time.
— *Sue Banducci*

Old

By the time we've made it, we've had it.
— *Malcolm Forbes*

Old

Old age is life's parody.
— *Simone de Beauvoir*

I'm growing fonder of my staff;
I'm growing dimmer in the eyes;
I'm growing fainter in my laugh;
I'm growing deeper in my sighs;
I'm growing careless of my dress;
I'm growing frugal of my gold;
I'm growing wise; I'm growing — yes —
I'm growing old.
— *John Godfrey Saxe*

*I*f not now, when?
— *Hillel the Elder*

*G*ather ye rosebuds while ye may,
Old Time is still a-flying,
And this same flower that smiles today
Tomorrow will be dying.
— *Robert Herrick*

*D*efer not till tomorrow to be wise,
Tomorrow's sun to thee may never rise.
— *William Congreve*

*N*othing is more responsible for the good old days
than a bad memory.
— *Franklin Adams*

*H*ow is it that our memory is good enough to retain
the least triviality that happens to us,
and yet not good enough to recollect
how often we have told it to the same person?
— *Duc de La Rochefoucauld*

I am so old I can remember when the air was clean
and sex was dirty.
— *George Burns*

*A*ge only matters when one is aging.
Now that I have arrived at a great age,
I might just as well be twenty.
— *Pablo Picasso*

*M*en are like wine. Some turn to vinegar,
but the best improve with age.
— *Pope John XXIII*

*T*he first forty years of life gives us the text;
the next thirty years supply the commentary.
— *Arthur Schopenhauer*

I don't feel eighty. In fact I don't feel anything till noon.
Then it's time for my nap.
— *Bob Hope*

*Y*ou know you're getting old
when you stoop to tie your shoes and
wonder what else you can do while you're down there.
— *George Burns*

*T*he only advantage of old age is that you can sing
while you brush your teeth.
— *Anonymous*

*M*iddle Age is when your age
starts to show around your middle.
— *Bob Hope*

*A*t another year
I would not boggle,
Except that when I jog
I joggle.
— *Ogden Nash*

I am as old as my tongue
and older than my teeth.
— *Jonathan Swift*

*M*y diseases are an asthma and a dropsy and,
what is less curable, seventy-five.
— *Samuel Johnson*

*T*here are so many ways of dying,
it is astonishing that any of us choose old age.
— *Beryl Bainbridge*

*A*n old man in love
is like a flower in winter.
— *Portuguese proverb*

*I*n love, as in other matters,
the young are just beginners.
— *Isaac Bashevis Singer*

*G*row old along with me!
The best is yet to be.
— *Robert Browning*

*D*on't rush,
eternity will wait.
— *Elliott Priest*

*E*njoy yourself;
it's later than you think.
— *Chinese proverb*

*S*hould we slow down because we are getting older,
or hurry up because we'll not get any younger?
— *Anonymous*

I used to dread getting older because I thought
I would not be able to do all the things I wanted to do.
But now that I am older I find I don't want to do them.
— *Nancy Astor (at eighty)*

❦

*W*hen you are about thirty-five years old,
something terrible always happens to music.
— *Steve Race*

❦

*T*here is only one thing wrong
with the younger generation —
a lot of us don't belong to it anymore.
— *Bernard Baruch*

$\mathcal{E}$yes that see do not grow old.
— *Nicaraguan proverb*

$\mathcal{M}$ore exquisite than any other
is the autumn rose.
— *Théodore Agrippa d'Aubigné*

*Y*outh is a silly, vapid state;
Old Age with fears and ills is rife;
This simple boon I beg of Fate —
A thousand years of Middle Life!
— *Carolyn Wells*

*M*iddle age is when anything new in the way you feel
is most likely a symptom.
— *Sidney Body*

*E*very twenty years,
the middle aged celebrate
the decade of their youth.
— *Gore Vidal*

I'd like to go on being thirty-five for a long time.
— *Margaret Thatcher (at fifty-four)*

*H*e decided to live forever,
or die in the attempt.
— *Joseph Heller*

They tell you that you lose your mind
when you grow older.
What they don't tell you is that you
won't miss it very much.
— *Malcolm Cowley*

At age fifty-eight I am in the prime of senility.
— *Joel C. Harris*

I'm sixty-five and I guess that puts me in with the geriatrics,
but if there were fifteen months in every year,
I'd only be forty-eight.
— *James Thurber*

*A*nd almost everyone when age,
Disease, or sorrows strike him,
Inclines to think there is a God,
Or something very like Him.
— *Arthur Hugh Clough*

*I*f you are sufficiently
irascible,
God might just decide
to wait.
— *Godfrey Just*

$\mathcal{T}$ime does not become sacred to us
until we have lived it.
— *John Burroughs*

$\mathcal{I}$f I had my life to live over,
I would pick more daisies.
— *Nadine Stair*

$\mathcal{T}$here is never enough time,
unless you're serving it.
— *Malcolm Forbes*

*Y*outh is a disease from which we all recover.
— *Dorothy Fuldheim*

*P*reparing for the worst is an activity
I have taken up since I turned thirty-five,
and the worst actually began to happen.
— *Delia Ephron*

*M*iddle age is when you're sitting at home
on Saturday night and the telephone rings
and you hope it isn't for you.
— *Ogden Nash*

$\mathcal{M}$iddle age: becoming like our parents
while fighting with our children.
— *Elliott Priest*

$\mathcal{W}$hoever is not a misanthrope at forty
can never have loved mankind.
— *Sebastien Chamfort*

$\mathcal{O}$f all the barbarous middle ages,
that which is most barbarous is the middle age of man.
— *Lord Byron*

*M*y age is as a lusty winter,
Frosty, but kindly.
— *William Shakespeare*

*H*ow beautifully the leaves grow old.
How full of light and colour are their last days.
— *John Burroughs*

*A*s a white candle
In a holy place
So is the beauty
Of an aged face.
— *Joseph Campbell*

*I*n the depth of winter,
I finally learned that within me
there lay an invincible summer.
— *Albert Camus*

*M*y eyes have seen much,
but they are not weary.
My ears have heard much,
but they thirst for more.
— *Rabindranath Tagore*

*W*e end in joy.
— *Theodore Roethke*

I advise you to go on living solely to enrage
those who are paying your annuities.
It is the only pleasure I have left.
— *Voltaire*

I have been dead
for two years,
but I don't choose
to have it known.
— *Lord Chesterfield*

$\mathcal{M}$ost women are not so young
as they are painted.
— *Sir Max Beerbohm*

$\mathcal{Y}$ou've heard of the three ages of man:
youth, middle age,
and "You're looking wonderful!"
— *Francis Joseph and Cardinal Spellman*

*W*rinkles should merely indicate
where smiles have been.
— *Mark Twain*

*W*ithin I do not find wrinkles and used heart,
but unspent youth.
— *Ralph Waldo Emerson (at sixty-one)*

*O*ld age takes away from us what we have inherited
and gives us what we have earned.
— *Gerald Brendan*

*A*fter thirty-five a man begins
to have thoughts about women;
before that age he has feelings.
— *Austin O'Malley*

❦

*O*ld age is a closed mind
and an open fly.
— *Anonymous*

❦

*A*s a matter of fact,
elderly people are not more contemptible
than anyone else.
— *Evelyn Waugh*

$\mathcal{O}$ne trouble with growing older
is that it gets progressively tougher
to find a famous historical figure
who didn't amount to much when he was your age.
— *Bill Vaughan*

$\mathcal{T}$he older they get,
the better they were when they were younger.
— *Jim Boutton*

Middle age: when the past was perfect,
and the present is tense.
— *Elliott Priest*

The closing years of life are like
the end of a masquerade party,
when the masks are dropped.
— *Arthur Schopenhauer*

We grow neither better nor
worse as we get old,
but more like ourselves.
— *May Lamberton Becker*

*A*s at seven, so at seventy.
— *Jewish proverb*

*A*ge does not make us childish, as they say.
It only finds us true children still.
— *Johann Wolfgang von Goethe*

*C*hildhood sometimes does pay
a second visit to man;
youth never.
— *Anna Jameson*

Seventy is wormwood.
Seventy is gall.
It is better to be seventy
Than not alive at all.
— *Phyllis McGinley*

🌿

Old age is the only disease
you don't look forward to being cured of.
— *Anonymous*

*W*ell, here I am thirty-eight,
Well, I certainly thought I'd have longer to wait.
You just stop in for a couple of beers,
And gosh, there go thirty-seven years.
— *Ogden Nash*

[*M*iddle age:] That vague time,
the time of regrets that resemble hopes,
of hopes that resemble regrets,
when youth has passed,
but old age has not yet arrived.
— *Ivan Sergeyevich Turgenev*

*O*ld age is a tyrant,
which forbids the pleasures of youth on pain of death.
— *Duc de La Rochefoucauld*

*I*f I'd known I was going to live so long,
I'd have taken better care of myself.
— *Leon Eldred*

*O*ld age needs so little,
but it needs that little so much.
— *Anonymous*

*I*t's not that I'm afraid to die.
I just don't want to be there when it happens.
— *Woody Allen*

*T*hey say such nice things about people
at their funerals it makes me sad
to realize that I'm going to miss mine
by just a few days.
— *Garrison Keillor*

The wine of youth does not always clear
with advancing years;
sometimes it grows turbid.
— *Carl Jung*

❦

Age mellows some people;
others it makes rotten.
— *Anonymous*

❦

Describing seventy as the golden age
is a modern form of alchemy.
— *Elliott Priest*

My parents didn't want to move to Florida,
but they turned sixty,
and it was the law.
— *Jerry Seinfeld*

Life is a country that the old have seen,
and lived in.
Those who have to travel through it
can only learn from them.
— *Joseph Joubert*

Old age is a good example of the journey
being better than the arrival.
— *Elliott Priest*

*O*ld age —
when actions creak louder than words.
— *Anonymous*

*A*dvanced old age is when you sit in a rocking chair
and can't get it going.
— *Anonymous*

*T*o get back my youth
I would do anything in the world,
except take exercise, get up early,
or be respectable.
— *Oscar Wilde*

King David and King Solomon
Led merry, merry lives,
With many, many lady friends
And many, many wives;
But when old age crept over them —
With many, many qualms,
King Solomon wrote the Proverbs,
And King David wrote the Psalms.
— *James B. Naylor*

*E*veryone is born a king,
and most people die in exile.
— *Oscar Wilde*

*T*hey are all gone into the world of light,
And I alone sit lingering here.
— *Henry Vaughan*

*L*ook back on time with kindly eyes,
He doubtless did his best;
How softly sinks his trembling sun
In human nature's west.
— *Emily Dickinson*

*W*hen you hit seventy, you eat better, you sleep sounder,
you feel more alive than when you were thirty.
Obviously, it's healthier to have women
on your mind than on your knees.
— *Maurice Chevalier*

A man is as old as he looks,
and if he only looks — he is old.
— *Anonymous*

*B*oys will be boys,
and so will a lot of middle-aged men.
— *Frank McKinney Hubbard*

*N*owadays most women grow old gracefully;
most men, disgracefully.
— *Helen Rowland*

*A*n evil name — a drawback at first —
sheds luster on old age.
— *Logan Pearsall Smith*

*G*rowing old — it's not nice,
but it's interesting.
— *August Strindberg*

My heart leaps up when I behold
A rainbow in the sky:
So was it when my life began;
So is it now I am a man;
So be it when I shall grow old,
Or let me die!
— *William Wordsworth*

The trick is to grow up
without growing old.
— *Frank Lloyd Wright*

*M*y interest is in the future because
I am going to spend the rest of my life there.
— *Charles F. Kettering*

I never think of the future.
It comes soon enough.
— *Albert Einstein*

*O*ld and young,
we are all on our last cruise.
— *Robert Louis Stevenson*

For a fool, old age is winter.
For a wise man, it is a time of harvest.
— *Jewish proverb*

*W*isdom doesn't always
show up with age.
Sometimes age shows up
all by itself.
— *Tom Wilson*

I am ready to meet my Maker.
Whether my Maker is prepared for the ordeal
of meeting me is another matter.
— *Winston Churchill (on his seventy-fifth birthday)*

🌱

*D*o not go gentle into that good night,
Old age should burn and rage at close of day;
Rage, rage, against the dying of the light.
— *Dylan Thomas*

🌱

I pray that I may seem,
though I die old,
a foolish, passionate man.
— *William Butler Yeats*

$\mathcal{E}$xperience. The wisdom that enables us
to recognize in an undesirable old acquaintance
the folly that we have already embraced.
— *Ambrose Bierce*

$\mathcal{T}$hou shouldst not have been old
till thou hadst been wise.
— *William Shakespeare*

$\mathcal{T}$he older I grow, the more I distrust
the familiar doctrine that age brings wisdom.
— *H. L. Mencken*

One should never make one's debut
with a scandal; one should reserve that
to give interest to one's old age.
— *Oscar Wilde*

I have my eighty-seventh birthday coming up
and people ask what I'd most appreciate getting.
I'll tell you: a paternity suit.
— *George Burns*

Time goes by: reputation increases,
ability declines.
— *Dag Hammarskjöd*

"*Y*ou are old, Father William," the young man said,
"And your hair has become very white;
And yet you incessantly stand on your head —
Do you think, at your age, it is right?"

"In my youth," Father William replied to his son,
"I feared it might injure the brain;
But, now that I'm perfectly sure I have none,
Why, I do it again and again."
— *Lewis Caroll*

*I*t's never to late to have a fling
For autumn is just as nice as spring
And it's never too late to fall in love.
— *Sandy Wilson*

*L*ove is like the
measles.
All the worse when it
comes late in life.
— *Douglas Jerrold*

*W*hen I was young I used to think that money
was the most important thing in life;
now that I am old, I know it is.
— *Oscar Wilde*

*F*rom birth to age eighteen, a girl needs good parents.
From eighteen to thirty-five, she needs good looks.
From thirty-five to fifty-five, she needs a good personality.
From fifty-five on, she needs good cash.
— *Sophie Tucker*

The young feel tired at the end of an action,
the old at the beginning.
— *T. S. Eliot*

Sex after ninety is like trying to shoot pool with a rope.
Even putting my cigar in its holder is a thrill.
— *George Burns*

Find an aim in life,
before you run out of ammunition.
— *Arnold Glasgow*

*W*hat's a man's age?
He must hurry more, that's all;
Cram in a day what his youth/
took a year to hold.
— *Robert Browning*

*W*e haven't the time to take our time.
— *Eugène Ionesco*

*T*ime goes, you say? Ah no!
Alas, Time stays, *we* go.
— *[Henry] Austin Dobson*

I refuse to admit I'm more than fifty-two
even if that does make my sons illegitimate.
— *Lady Nancy Astor*

I will never be old.
To me, old age is always
fifteen years older than I am.
— *Bernard Baruch*

*T*here is one thing about baldness:
it's neat.
— *Don Herold*

I beg your pardon,
I didn't recognize you —
I've changed a lot.
— *Oscar Wilde*

*M*iddle age: that point in life where,
when your wife tells you to pull in
your stomach, you already have.
— *Anonymous*

*T*ime is a dressmaker
specializing in alterations.
— *Faith Baldwin*

*T*ime is a great teacher,
but unfortunately it kills all its pupils.
— *Hector Berlioz*

*T*ime is a friend,
he will make us old.
— *Sara Teasdale*

When I remember bygone days
I think how evening follows morn;
So many I loved were not yet dead,
So many I love were not yet born.
— *Ogden Nash*

The past is a foreign country;
they do things differently there.
— *L. P. Barthartley*

What youth deemed crystal,
age finds out was dew.
— *Robert Browning*

*M*iddle age is when you have more yesterdays
than tomorrows.
— *Bill Clinton*

*F*orty is the old age of youth,
fifty is the youth of old age.
— *Victor Hugo*

*M*en at forty
Learn to close softly
The doors to rooms they will not be
Coming back to.
— *Donald Justice*

The denunciation of the young
is a necessary part of the hygiene of older people,
and greatly assists the circulation of their blood.
— *Logan Pearsall Smith*

The old believe everything,
the middle-aged suspect everything,
the young know everything.
— *Oscar Wilde*

Blessed are the young,
for they shall inherit the national debt.
— *Herbert Hoover*

I was born in 1962. True.
And the room next to me was *1963* . . .
— *Joan Rivers*

*T*ime and tide wait for no man,
but time always stands still
for a woman of thirty.
— *Robert Frost*

I don't consider myself bald.
I'm simply taller than my hair.
— *Tom Sharp*

Middle-aged life is merry, and I love to lead it,
But there comes a day when your eyes are all right/
but your arm isn't long enough to hold/
the telephone book where you can read it.
  — Ogden Nash

One thing that bifocals do give you is hindsight.
  — Godfrey Just

*M*iddle age is the best time,
if we can escape the fatty degeneration
of the conscience
which often sets about at fifty.
— *W. R. Inge*

*T*he lovely thing about being forty
is that you can appreciate
twenty-five-year-old men more.
— *Colleen McCullough*

*A*t middle age the soul should be
opening up like a rose,
not closing up like a cabbage.
— *John Andrew Holmes*

A man could retire to a comfortable old age
if he could dispose of his experience
for what it cost him.
— *Anonymous*

*C*ast me not off in the time of old age;
forsake me not when my strength faileth.
— *Old Testament*

*W*hen one has reached eighty-one,
one likes to sit back and let the world turn by itself,
without trying to push it.
— *Sean O'Casey*

*I*f I had my life to live again,
I'd make the same mistakes — only sooner.
— *Tallulah Bankhead*

I believe that one has to be seventy
before one is full of courage.
The young are always half-hearted.
— *D. H. Lawrence*

I speak the truth, not my fill of it,
but as much as I dare speak;
and I dare to do so a little more as I grow old.
— *Michel Eyquem de Montaigne*

*O*ld fools are babes again.
— *William Shakespeare*

I delight in men over seventy,
they always offer one
the devotion of a lifetime.
— *Oscar Wilde's Mrs. Allonby*

*W*hat I wouldn't give to be seventy again!
— *Oliver Wendell Holmes, Jr.*
(at ninety-two, after seeing a pretty girl)

*I*t is not white hair that engenders wisdom.
— *Menander (342-292 B.C.)*

*H*e who devotes sixteen hours a day
to hard study
may become as wise at sixty
as he thought himself at twenty.
— *Mary Wilson Little*

*A*fter the age of eighty,
all contemporaries are friends.
— *Duchesse de Dino*

I've never known a person to live
to be one hundred and ten
and be remarkable for anything else.
— *Josh Billings*

*I*n my youth I thought of writing
a satire on mankind,
but now in my age I think I should write
an apology for them.
— *Horace Wapella*

*T*he man who is a pessimist before forty-eight
knows too much.
The man who is an optimist after forty-eight
knows too little.
— *Mark Twain*

*A*n optimist is someone
who thinks the future is uncertain.
— *Anonymous*

*G*o uphill as fast as you please;
but go downhill slowly.
— *Josh Billings*

*G*od gave us memories
so that we might have roses in December.
— *James Matthew Barrie*

❦

*R*ecollection is the only paradise
from which we cannot be turned out.
— *Jean Paul Richter*

❦

*E*very man's memory
is his private literature.
— *Aldous Huxley*

*Y*outh is a blunder, manhood a struggle,
old age a regret.
— *Benjamin Disraeli*

*L*ife is like playing a
violin solo in public
and learning the instrument
as one goes on.
— *Baron Laden*

*T*he young man who has not wept is a savage,
and the old man who will not laugh is a fool.
— *George Santayana*

*W*e should live and learn;
but by the time we've learned it is too late to live.
— *Carolyn Wells*

*N*o person is ever too old to yearn.
— *Addison Miner*

*W*hen I was young there was no respect for the young,
and now that I am old there is no respect for the old.
I missed out coming and going.
— *J. B. Priestley*

*I*t costs a great deal to be reasonable.
It costs youth.
— *Madame de la Fayette*

*Y*outh, large, lusty, loving — youth/
full of grace, force, fascination,
Do you know that Old Age may come after you/
with equal grace, force, fascination?
— *Walt Whitman*

*F*un is like life insurance:
the older you get, the more it costs.
— *Frank McKinney Hubbard*

*T*ime is money,
but you are never sure of your balance.
— *Anonymous*

*I*t is not true that life is one damn thing after another;
it's one damn thing over and over.
— *Edna St. Vincent Millar*

*M*iddle age begins with the first mortgage
and ends when you drop dead.
— *Herb Caen*

*T*ime flies.
We stumble.
— *Godfrey Just*

*C*hildren are a great comfort in your old age —
and they help you reach it faster, too.
— *Lionel Kauffman*

*S*etting a good example for children
takes all the fun out of middle age.
— *William Feather*

*I*f you want to find your lost youth —
cut off his allowance.
— *Anonymous*

*W*hen we are out of sympathy with the young,
then I think our work in this world is over.
— *George MacDonald*

*O*ld people are always absorbed in something.
Usually themselves.
— *Sidney and Beatrice Webb*

*W*e are tomorrow's past.
— *Mary Webb*

Old age is when you know all the answers
but nobody asks you the questions.
— *Bert K. Smith*

❦

At twenty we worry about what others think of us.
At forty we don't care what others think of us.
At sixty we discover they haven't
been thinking about us at all.
— *Anonymous*

*Y*outh had been a habit of hers for so long that
she could not part with it.
— *Rudyard Kipling*

A hair in the head
is worth two in the brush.
— *Oliver Herford*

*M*iddle age is nature's way of showing
a sense of humour.
— *Anonymous*

*M*iddle age is when the best exercise
is one of discretion.
— *Laurence J. Peter*

*A*fter a certain age, if you don't wake up
aching in every joint,
you are probably dead.
— *Tommy Mein*

I smoke cigars because at my age if I don't have something
to hang onto I might fall down.
— *George Burns*

*W*hen you are through changing,
you are through.
— *Anonymous*

*T*he man who is too old to learn
was probably always too old to learn.
— *Henry Haskins*

*I*t takes a long time to become young.
— *Pablo Picasso*

*A*s soon as a man acquires fairly good sense,
it is said that he is an old fogy.
— *Ed Howe*

*T*he teeth of wisdom
may well be false.
— *Elliott Priest*

*M*any a man that can't direct
you to a corner drugstore
when young,
will get a respectful hearing
when age has further
impaired his mind.
— *Finley P. Dunne*

I don't want to achieve immortality through my work.
I want to achieve it through not dying.
— *Woody Allen*

*M*illions long for immortality
who do not know what to do with themselves
on a rainy Sunday afternoon.
— *Susan Ertz*

*A*h, well, there is just this world and then the next,
and then all our troubles will be over.
— *L. O. Asquith, quoting an old lady*

*O*ld age is like everything else.
To make a success of it
you've got to start young.
— *Fred Astaire*

*W*e must not take the faults of our youth
into our old age;
for old age
brings with it its own defects.
— *Johann Wolfgang von Goethe*

*L*ife is short, but it is long enough
for any man who wants to be ruined.
— *Josh Billings*

*Y*ou know you're getting old
when the candles cost more than the cake.
— *Bob Hope*

*T*he hardest years in life are those
between ten and seventy.
— *Helen Hayes (at eighty-three)*

*W*hen a woman tells you her age,
it's all right to looked surprised,
but don't scowl.
— *Wilson Mizner*

The gardener's rule applies to youth and age:
when young sow wild oats,
but when old grow sage.
— *Lord Byron*

*B*ut though an
old man,
I am but a young
gardener.
— *Thomas Jefferson*

*O*ld minds are like old horses;
you must exercise them if you wish
to keep them in working order.
— *John Quincy Adams*

*A*fter a certain age some people's minds close up;
they live on their intellectual fat.
— *William Lyon Phelps*

I think, therefore I still am.
— *Elliott Priest*

*E*veryone is as God made him,
unless he has managed to make things worse.
— *Miguel de Cervantes*

*A*t age fifty,
every man has the face he deserves.
— *George Orwell*

*A*ge comes in on little crow's feet.
— *Anonymous*

*O*ld age: the crown of life,
our play's last act.
— *Marcus Tullius Cicero (106–43 B.C.)*

*E*ven a great feast
has a last course.
— *Chinese proverb*

*T*he four stages of man are
infancy, childhood, adolescence,
and obsolescence.
— *Art Linkletter*

❧

*A*fter seventy,
it's patch, patch, patch.
— *Jimmy Stewart*

❧

A man is as old as his arteries.
— *Thomas Sydenham (1624–89)*

The evening of life
brings with it its lamps.
— *Joseph Joubert*